Sugar Free Dessert Cookbook

Healthy Sugar Free Dessert Recipes For Losing Weight

Table of Contents

Introduction

Plenty of research has shown that reducing sugar in your diet is key for losing weight, lowering your risk for cancer and reducing inflammation among many other health benefits. With all these wonderful benefits that reducing sugar has on your health, you may wonder why most people do not cut sugar out of their diet. There is a easy yet troubling explanation for this problem, and it is that sugar is very addictive.

Like quitting smoking, eliminating your sugar cravings can be extremely difficult. This baking cookbook is designed to help you beat your sugar cravings, by giving you delicious sugar free cake, cookie and pie recipes. These recipes will make you forget that you are on a sugar free diet! Good luck, we hope you enjoy these sugar free baking and dessert recipes.

Chapter 1: Sugar Free Cake And Square Recipes

Sugar Free Butterscotch Brownies

Ingredients

2 1/4 cups all-purpose flour

1 teaspoon baking powder

1/2 teaspoon salt

1 cup (2 sticks) butter or margarine, softened

3/4 cup packed Splenda Brown Sugar Blend

1 tablespoon vanilla extract

2 large eggs

1 2/3 cups (11-ounce package) sugar free butterscotch flavored chips - divided use

1/2 cup chopped pecans

Directions

Preheat oven to 350°F (175°C).

Combine flour, baking powder and salt in medium bowl. Beat butter, Splenda Brown Sugar Blend and vanilla extract in large mixer bowl until creamy. Beat in eggs. Gradually beat in flour mixture. Stir in 1 cup butterscotch chips and nuts. Spread into ungreased 13x9x2-inch baking pan. Sprinkle with remaining chips.

Bake for 30 to 40 minutes or until wooden pick inserted in center comes out clean. Cool in pan on wire rack. Cut into bars.

Banana Chocolate Cake

Ingredients

3 large eggs

1/4 cup butter

1 teaspoon ground cinnamon

1/2 cup unsweetened applesauce

1 cup fresh mashed banana

2 cups ground almond

1/4 cup water

2 teaspoon baking powder

1 teaspoon baking soda

Directions

Preheat oven to 350F.

Grease a 9 x 13 baking dish. In a bowl, beat banana and butter until creamy, then beat in water and applesauce. In another bowl, beat eggs until foamy and pour eggs into banana mixture.

In a separate bowl blend flour powder soda cinnamon then add banana mixture and beat until smooth. Pour into baking dish and bake in oven for 20 minutes (or until toothpick comes out clean).

Coconut Walnut Bars

Ingredients

2 large eggs

1 cup Equal (sugar substitute)

1/4 teaspoon maple flavoring

1/2 cup margarine, melted

1 teaspoon vanilla extract

1/2 cup all-purpose flour

1 teaspoon baking powder

1/4 teaspoon salt

1 cup unsweetened coconut, finely chopped

1/2 cup chopped walnuts

1/2 cup raisins

Directions

Beat eggs, Equal and maple flavoring in medium bowl; mix in margarine and vanilla. Combine flour, baking powder and salt in small bowl; stir into egg mixture. Mix in coconut, walnuts, and raisins. Spread batter evenly in greased 8-inch square baking pan.

Bake in preheated 350°F (175°C) oven until browned and toothpick inserted in center comes out clean, about 20 minutes.

Cool in pan on wire rack; cut into squares.

Pumpkin Chocolate Chip Bars

Ingredients

1 1/3 cups all-purpose flour

1/4 cup Splenda Brown Sugar Blend

1/2 cup Splenda Sugar Blend - divided use

1 cup old-fashioned oats

1/2 cup chopped walnuts or pecans

3/4 cup light margarine

1 (8-ounce) container fat-free cream cheese

3 large eggs

1 (15-ounce) can pumpkin

1 tablespoon pumpkin pie spice

1 cup sugar free mini chocolate chips

Directions

Bake in a preheated oven at 350°F (175°C). Line a 13X9 pan with foil and spray with a non-stick cooking spray. Set aside.

Combine flour, Splenda Brown Sugar Blend, half of the Splenda Sugar Blend, oats and walnuts. Cut in the margarine with a fork until the mixture is crumbly.

Press all but one cup of the crust mixture into the bottom of the prepared pan. Bake for 15 minutes. Allow to cool.

Beat cream cheese, eggs, the remaining half of the Splenda Sugar Blend, the pumpkin and the pumpkin pie spice until it is well blended.

Pour the cream cheese mixture over the pre-baked crust and sprinkle with the 1 cup of remaining crust and the chocolate chips.

Bake for 25 minutes or until set. Lift from pan to cool.

Yellow Applesauce Cake

Ingredients

1 package sugar free yellow cake mix

1 cup non fat milk

1/3 cup unsweetened apple sauce

3 large egg whites

1/2 package cool whip light

Directions

Mix cake mix, milk, applesauce, and egg whites together and beat about 2 minutes on medium speed.

Pour in 9x13 cake pan and bake at 325 degrees for 35- 40 minutes. Let cool frost with cool whip light.

Apple Caramel Cheesecake

Ingredients

1 (21-ounce) can apple pie filling (no sugar added)

1 (6-ounce) reduced fat graham cracker pie crust

2 (8-ounce) containers nonfat cream cheese, at room temperature

1/3 cup Splenda Granulated No Calorie Sweetener

1 teaspoon vanilla extract

2 large eggs

1/3 cup chopped pecans

1/4 cup sugar free caramel sauce

Directions

Preheat oven to 350°F (175°C). Reserve 3/4 cup of apple pie filling.

Spoon remaining pie filling into crust. In a large bowl, combine cream cheese, Splenda Granulated Sweetener, and vanilla. Beat until smooth, then beat in eggs one at a time. Pour over apple filling in crust.

Bake in a preheated oven at 350°F (175°C) for 35 minutes, or until center is set. Remove from oven, and cool to room temperature.

In a small saucepan melt caramel with reserved apple filling. Arrange apple slices around outside edge of cheesecake. Spread caramel sauce evenly over the top.

Sprinkle with chopped pecans. Chill until ready to serve.

Marble Cake

Ingredients

Cake:

3 tablespoons Dutch process cocoa

1 tablespoon Splenda Sugar Blend for Baking

1/4 teaspoon baking soda

2 1/2 tablespoons hot water

2 cups sifted cake flour

1/2 cup Splenda Sugar Blend for Baking

2 1/2 teaspoons baking powder

1/4 teaspoon salt

1/2 cup butter

2 large eggs, lightly beaten

2/3 cup milk

1 teaspoon vanilla extract

Directions

Preheat oven to 325°F (160°C). Grease and flour a 6-cup Bundt pan or an 8x4-inch loaf pan. Set aside.

Combine cocoa, 1 tablespoon Splenda Sugar Blend for Baking, and baking soda; gradually stir in hot water to form a paste. Set aside.

Combine flour, Splenda Sugar Blend for Baking, baking powder, and salt in a large mixing bowl. Cut butter into flour mixture with a fork or a pastry blender until crumbly. Cover mixing bowl with a clean tea towel to prevent spattering.

Combine eggs, milk, and vanilla in a small mixing bowl; add 1/3 of the egg mixture to flour mixture. Beat at low speed of an electric mixer until blended.

Beat at medium speed for 30 seconds or until batter is smooth, stopping to scrape down sides of bowl. Repeat procedure 2 times.

Set aside half of the batter. Add cocoa mixture to remaining batter, beating at low speed until blended. Alternate light and dark batters by tablespoonfuls into prepared pan. Gently swirl batters with a knife to create a marble effect.

Bake 45 to 50 minutes or until a wooden pick inserted in center comes out clean. Cool in pan on a wire rack 10 minutes. Remove from pan; cool completely on a wire rack.

Almond Raspberry Bars

Ingredients

2 cups all-purpose flour

1/2 cup Equal

1/8 teaspoon salt

8 tablespoons cold stick butter or margarine, cut into pieces

1 large egg

2 tablespoons water

1 teaspoon grated lemon peel

1 (10-ounce) jar seedless raspberry spreadable fruit

3 tablespoons toasted sliced almonds

Directions

Combine flour, Equal and salt in medium bowl. Cut in butter with pastry blender until mixture resembles coarse crumbs.

Stir in egg, water and lemon peel. Mixture will be crumbly.

Press mixture evenly onto bottom of well-sprayed 8x8-inch square baking pan. Bake in preheated 350°F (175°C) oven 12 to 15 minutes or until edges of crust are lightly browned.

Remove pan from oven and spread raspberry fruit over top. Sprinkle with almonds. Return to oven, and bake an additional 10 to 12 minutes or until raspberry fruit is bubbly. Cool completely on wire rack. Cut into bars.

Store in airtight containers at room temperature.

Chocolate Brownies

Ingredients

1 cup butter spread, melted

2 cups granular sucralose sweetener

1/2 cup unsweetened cocoa powder

1 teaspoon vanilla extract

4 eggs

1 cup all-purpose flour

1/2 teaspoon baking powder

1/2 teaspoon salt

Directions

Preheat oven to 350 degrees F (175 degrees C). Grease a 9x13-inch baking pan.

Mix melted butter spread, sweetener, cocoa powder, vanilla extract, eggs, flour, baking powder, and salt together in a large bowl. Pour into the prepared pan.

Bake in the preheated oven until a toothpick inserted into the center comes out clean, about 20 minutes.

Oatmeal Apricot Squares

Ingredients

1 1/4 cups all-purpose flour

3/4 cup quick or old-fashioned oats, uncooked

1/2 cup Equal

1/2 teaspoon ground cinnamon

1/4 teaspoon baking powder

1/8 teaspoon salt

1/2 cup cold stick butter

2 tablespoons water

1 teaspoon vanilla extract

3/4 cup apricot spreadable fruit

Directions

Combine flour, oats, Equal, cinnamon, baking powder and salt. Cut in butter with a pastry blender until mixture is very fine in texture and begins to stick together slightly. Stir in water and vanilla until well blended.

Reserve 3/4 cup flour mixture. Press remaining mixture firmly and evenly onto bottom of lightly sprayed 8-inch square baking pan. Bake in preheated 375°F oven 12 to 15 minutes or until mixture is lightly browned at edge.

Remove from oven and spread with fruit. Sprinkle with reserved flour mixture, pressing gently into fruit.

Bake an additional 20 to 25 minutes or until flour mixture is lightly browned on top. Cool completely on wire rack. Cut into squares.

Store in airtight containers at room temperature.

Raspberry Lemon Bars

Ingredients

Crust:
3/4 cup Splenda Granular

3/4 cup all-purpose flour

1/4 cup light butter

Pinch of salt

Filling:
2 tablespoons all-purpose flour

1 1/4 cups Splenda Granular

1/2 cup egg substitute (or 2 large eggs)

1/2 cup half-and-half

1/2 cup fresh lemon juice

1 tablespoon grated fresh lemon peel

1/4 cup reduced sugar raspberry preserves

Directions

Preheat oven to 350°F (175°C). Spray an 8x8x2-inch-baking pan generously with butter flavored nonstick spray. Set aside.

Mix together flour, Splenda Granular and salt in a medium sized mixing bowl. Cut in light butter until the mixture is crumbly, like a streusel topping. Do Not over mix. Press dough into prepared baking pan.

Bake in preheated oven 15 to 20 minutes or until lightly browned.

Place Splenda Granular and flour in a medium sized mixing bowl. Stir well. Add egg substitute and half-and-half. Stir until blended. Slowly add lemon juice while stirring constantly. Add lemon peel.

Stir raspberry preserves until they loosen up. Spread evenly over warm crust.

Gently pour lemon mixture over preserves. Bake in preheated oven 20 to 25 minutes or until set. Remove from oven and allow to cool before placing in refrigerator.

Chill in refrigerator 2 hours before serving.

Orange Coffee Cake

Ingredients

2-1/4 cups Bisquick

1/2 teaspoon baking powder

1/2 cup granulated Splenda

1/2 tsp. baking soda

Two packets sweetener

Granulated sugar substitute

1/4 teaspoon ground ginger

1 tablespoon orange extract

1/4 cup skim buttermilk

1/2 cup unsalted reduced-calorie margarine

1/4 cup liquid egg substitute

3/4 teaspoon ground cinnamon

2 tablespoons orange juice

Directions

Preheat oven to 350F.

In a large bowl, combine bisquick, Splenda, sweetener and orange extract. With a pastry blender or two knives used scissor fashion, cut in margarine until mixture resembles coarse crumbs. Remove 1/2-cup and set aside. To remaining mixture add cinnamon, baking powder, baking soda and ginger.

In another small bowl, whisk together buttermilk, egg substitute and orange juice. Add to crumb mixture in large bowl; mix until just combined. Spray a oval casserole pan with non-stick cooking spray.

Spread batter evenly into the pan. Sprinkle reserved crumbs on top of batter. Bake 35-40 minutes or until toothpick inserted in center comes out clean.

Cool on rack for 15 minutes. Invert cake onto rack and cool completely.

Walnut Brownies

Ingredients

½ cup margarine

¼ cup unsweetened cocoa powder

2 eggs

1 cup Splenda granular

¾ cup all-purpose flour

⅛ teaspoon salt

¼ cup skim milk

½ cup chopped walnuts

Directions

Preheat oven to 350F°.

Spray Pam and flour an 8x8-inch pan. In a small saucepan, over medium heat, melt margarine and cocoa together, stirring occasionally until smooth.

Remove from heat and set aside to cool. In a large bowl, beat eggs until frothy.

Stir in Splenda. Combine the flour and salt; stir into the egg mixture then mix in the cocoa and margarine.

Finally stir in the 1/4 cup of milk and if desired, the walnuts. Pour into the prepared pan bake for 25-30 minutes in the preheated oven.

Test with a toothpick for doneness. Let cool and then cut into squares.

Lime Cheesecake

Ingredients

Crust:
1 1/4 cups graham cracker crumbs

1/4 cup Splenda Granulated No Calorie Sweetener

3 tablespoons butter, melted

Filling:
2 (8 ounce) packages cream cheese

1 (8 ounce) fat-free cream cheese

1 1/4 cups Splenda Granulated No Calorie Sweetener

4 large eggs

1 1/2 tablespoons lime juice

1 pinch salt

Directions
Preheat oven to 350°F (175°C). Spray a 9-inch springform pan with nonstick cooking spray. Set aside.

Combine graham cracker crumbs, Splenda Granulated Sweetener and melted butter in a small bowl. Press on bottom and up sides of prepared pan.

Bake 10 minutes. Remove from oven and cool on a wire rack.

Beat regular and fat free cream cheese together at high speed with a mixer until creamy; gradually add Splenda Granulated Sweetener, mixing well. Add eggs, one at a time, beating just until each one is incorporated. Add lime juice and a pinch of salt, beat until smooth. Pour into prepared crust.

Bake 50 to 60 minutes or until mixture is almost set, and slightly firm to the touch. Run a knife around edge of pan to release sides, and help prevent cracking. Cool to room temperature on a wire rack; cover and chill at least 8 hours.

Raisin Squares

Ingredients

1 cup raisins

½ cup water

¼ cup margarine

1 teaspoon cinnamon

½ teaspoon ground nutmeg

1 cup all-purpose flour

1 large egg, lightly beaten

¾ cup unsweetened applesauce

Splenda, equivalent to 1 tablespoon sugar

1 teaspoon baking soda

¼ teaspoon vanilla extract

Directions

In a saucepan over medium heat, cook raisins, water, margarine, cinnamon and nutmeg until margarine is melted; continue cooking for 3 minutes. Let cool.

Add all remaining ingredients and mix well. Spread into an 8-inch square pan coated with nonstick cooking spray.

Bake at 350F° for 20-25 minutes or until lightly browned.

Chapter 2: Sugar Free Pie Recipes

Blueberry Pie

Ingredients

9 inches double crust, pie

1 egg

1 tablespoon water

5 cups fresh blueberries

1 ¾ cups Splenda sugar substitute

4 tablespoons all-purpose flour

1 teaspoon cinnamon

1 teaspoon allspice

1 dash salt

2 tablespoons lemon juice

3 tablespoons unsalted butter, cut in small pieces

Directions

Pre heat oven 400 F.

Mix together egg and water to make a egg wash for the crust.

Mix together in a bowl blueberries, Splenda, flour, cinnamon, allspice, salt, then pour into prepared pie crust. Drizzle lemon juice over mixture then drop butter on top of mixture.

Add top crust, cut slits in top to vent and brush with egg wash. Cut slits in top crust to vent and bake for 45-50 minutes.

Cool at least 2 hours before serving.

Cherry Pie

Ingredients

1 (15-ounce) package refrigerated pie crusts

2 (14.5-ounce) cans pitted tart red cherries, undrained

2/3 cup Splenda

1/4 cup cornstarch

2 teaspoons fresh lemon juice

1/4 teaspoon almond extract

Directions

Preheat oven to 375°F (190°C).

Unfold 1 pie crust; press out fold lines. Fit pie crust into a 9-inch pie plate according to package directions. Drain cherries, reserving 1 cup juice; set fruit aside.

Combine Splenda and cornstarch in a medium saucepan; gradually stir reserved juice into Splenda mixture. Cook over medium heat, stirring constantly, until mixture begins to boil. Boil 1 minute, stirring constantly. Remove from heat; stir in lemon juice, and almond extract.

Fold in reserved cherries; cool slightly. Spoon mixture into pastry shell.

Unfold remaining pie crust; press out fold lines. Roll to 1-inch thickness. Place over filling; fold edges under and crimp. Cut slits in top to allow steam to escape.

Bake 40 to 50 minutes or until crust is golden. Cover edges with aluminum foil to prevent over browning, if necessary. Cool on a wire rack one hour before serving.

Berry Pie

Ingredients

1 (15-ounce) package refrigerated pie crusts

1 (14.5-ounce) can pitted tart red cherries, undrained

1 (12-ounce) package frozen raspberries, thawed

1 cup fresh blueberries or frozen blueberries, thawed

1 cup Splenda

1/4 cup cornstarch

2 tablespoons butter

Directions

Preheat oven to 375°F (190°C).

Unroll and fit one pie crust into a 9-inch pie plate; set aside.

Drain cherries, raspberries, and blueberries (if frozen), reserving 1 cup of the juices. Set berries and juice aside.

Combine Splenda and cornstarch in a medium saucepan; gradually stir in reserved juice. Cook over medium heat, stirring constantly, until mixture begins to boil. Boil 1 minute, stirring constantly. Stir in butter and reserved fruit. Cool slightly and spoon mixture into pie shell.

Unroll remaining pie crust; roll to 1/8-inch thickness: place over filling. Fold edges under and crimp. Cut slits in top to allow steam to escape.

Bake 40 to 45 minutes or until crust is golden. Cover edges with aluminum foil to prevent excessive browning, if necessary. Cool on a wire rack. Serve with a scoop of frozen low-fat vanilla yogurt, if desired.

Rhubarb Strawberry Pie

Ingredients

Pastry for single-crust 9-inch pie

3 cups 1-inch rhubarb pieces or 1 (16-ounce) package frozen unsweetened rhubarb, thawed, undrained

3/4 cup water

1/4 cup all-purpose flour

3 tablespoons cornstarch

2 tablespoons lemon juice

3 cups sliced strawberries

1 2/3 cups Equal (sugar substitute)

1/4 teaspoon ground nutmeg

Directions

Roll pastry on floured surface into circle 1-inch larger than inverted 9-inch pie plate. Ease pastry into plate; trim and flute edge. Pierce bottom and side of pastry with fork.

Bake in preheated 375°F (190°C) oven 10 to 12 minutes or until pastry is golden. Cool on wire rack.

Cook rhubarb in large covered saucepan over medium heat 5 minutes or until rhubarb releases liquid. Combine water, flour, cornstarch and lemon juice. Stir into rhubarb.

Heat to boiling. Reduce heat and simmer, uncovered, 3 to 5 minutes or until mixture is thickened and rhubarb is almost tender, stirring frequently. Stir in strawberries. Cook 2 to 3 minutes longer.

Stir Equal and nutmeg into fruit mixture. Spoon into baked crust.

Bake in 350°F (175°C) oven 40 to 45 minutes or until bubbly. Cover edge of crust with aluminum foil if browning too quickly. Cool on wire rack. Serve warm.

Pecan Pie

Ingredients

3 eggs

5 teaspoons equal (sugar substitute)

1 cup sugar free syrup

⅓ cup butter, melted

1 cup pecan halves

Pastry for 9" pie

Directions

Preheat oven to 350 degrees F. Mix eggs and sugar.

Stir in the breakfast syrup and melted butter. Stir in the pecan halves. Line a 9-inch pie pan with the pie dough.

Pour in the pecan pie filling mixture. Bake for 25 minutes with edges covered with foil.

Remove foil from the edges and bake for another 25 minutes. Cool on a wire rack.

Pineapple Banana Pie

Ingredients

Pastry for single crust 9-inch pie

2 (8-ounce each) packages reduced-fat cream cheese, softened

1/2 cup Equal

1 (8-ounce) container light whipped topping, thawed if frozen

1 (8-ounce) can crushed pineapple, well drained

1/4 cup flaked coconut - divided use

1/2 teaspoon rum extract

2 medium ripe bananas, cut into 1/2-inch thick slices

1 tablespoon chopped pecans

Directions

Preheat oven to 375°F (190°C).

Roll pastry on floured surface into circle 1-inch larger than inverted 9-inch pie plate. Ease pastry into plate; trim and flute edge. Pierce side and bottom of pastry with tines of a fork. Bake 10 to 12 minutes or until lightly browned. Cool completely on wire rack.

Meanwhile, beat cream cheese and Equal in mixing bowl on medium speed of mixer until smooth and well combined. Gradually mix in whipped topping, pineapple, 3 tablespoons coconut and rum extract.

Place half of cream cheese mixture over pie crust. Arrange banana slices in single layer. Top with remaining cream cheese mixture.

36

Sprinkle top of pie with remaining 1 tablespoon coconut and chopped pecans. Refrigerate 2 to 3 hours before serving.

Apple Pie

Ingredients

Pastry for double-crust 9-inch pie

3 tablespoons cornstarch

1 cup Equal (sugar substitute)

3/4 teaspoon ground cinnamon

1/4 teaspoon ground nutmeg

1/4 teaspoon salt

8 cups peeled, cored, sliced Granny Smith

Directions

Roll 1/2 the pastry on floured surface into circle 1-inch larger than inverted 9-inch pie plate. Ease pastry into plate.

Combine cornstarch, Equal, cinnamon, nutmeg and salt. Sprinkle over apples in large bowl and toss to coat. Arrange apples in pie crust.

Roll remaining pastry into circle large enough to fit top of pie. Place over apples. Seal edges, trim and flute. Cut a few slits in top of pastry to allow steam to escape. Bake in preheated 400°F oven 40 to 50 minutes or until crust is golden and apples are tender.

Cool on wire rack. Serve warm or at room temperature.

Chocolate Pie

Ingredients

⅓ cup cocoa or 2 ounces unsweetened chocolate, chopped

¾ teaspoon liquid stevia

¼ cup cornstarch

¼ teaspoon salt

3 ¼ cups milk

1 ½ teaspoons vanilla

1 (9 inch) baked pie shells

whipped cream

Directions

In a saucepan, mix together cocoa, stevia, cornstarch and salt. Stir milk in gradually.

Cook over medium heat, stirring constantly, until mixture boils; boil 1 minute. Remove from heat. Blend in vanilla.

Cool 10 minutes. Pour into pie shell; refrigerate. Top with whipped cream before serving if desired.

Classic Pumpkin Pie

Ingredients

2 eggs

1 (15 ounce) can pumpkin

¾ cup Splenda granular

½ teaspoon salt

1 teaspoon cinnamon

½ teaspoon ginger

¼ teaspoon clove

1 (12 ounce) can evaporated milk

1 -9 inch unbaked pie shell

Directions

Pre-heat oven to 425 F.

Combine all ingredients (except pie crust) in a bowl and mix well. Pour mixture into pie crust. Bake 15 minute at 425F.

Reduce heat to 350F and bake 45 more minutes. Cool and garnish with whipped cream.

Cranberry Apple Pie

Ingredients

Pie Crust
1 (15-ounce) package refrigerated pie crusts

Filling
1/2 cup Splenda

1 tablespoon all-purpose flour

1/2 teaspoon ground cinnamon

4 large Granny Smith Apples, peeled, cored and sliced

1 cup fresh or frozen cranberries

Directions
Preheat oven to 400°F (205°C).

Unfold 1 pie crust; press out fold lines. Fit pie crust into a 9-inch pie plate according to package directions.

Combine Splenda, flour, and cinnamon in a large bowl; add apples and cranberries, tossing gently. Spoon mixture into pie crust.

Unfold remaining pie crust; press out fold lines. Roll to 1/8-inch thickness. Place over filling; fold edges under and crimp. Cut slits in top to allow steam to escape.

Bake 40 to 50 minutes or until crust is golden. Cover edges with aluminum foil to prevent over-browning, if necessary. Cool on a wire rack one hour before serving.

Creamy Strawberry Pie

Ingredients

1 1/4 cups reduced-fat graham cracker crumbs

5 tablespoons margarine, melted

2 tablespoons + 1/4 cup + 1/2 cup Equal (divided)

1 (8-ounce) package reduced-fat cream cheese, softened

1 teaspoon vanilla extract

1 cup cold water

2 tablespoons cornstarch

1 (0.3-ounce) package sugar-free strawberry gelatin

1 pint strawberries, hulled, sliced

8 tablespoons frozen light whipped topping

Directions

Mix graham cracker crumbs, margarine and 2 tablespoon Equal in an 8-inch pie pan; pat evenly on bottom and side of pan. Bake in a preheated oven at 350°F (175°C) until lightly browned, 6 to 8 minutes. Cool.

Beat cream cheese, vanilla, and 1/4 cup Equal in small bowl until fluffy; spread evenly in bottom of crust.

Mix cold water and cornstarch in small saucepan; heat to boiling, whisking constantly until thickened, about 1 minute. Add gelatin and 1/2 cup Equal, whisking until gelatin is dissolved. Cool 10 minutes.

Arrange half of the strawberries over the cream cheese; spoon half the gelatin mixture over strawberries. Arrange remaining strawberries over pie and spoon remaining gelatin mixture over.

Refrigerate until pie is set and chilled, 1 to 2 hours. Serve with whipped topping, if desired.

Chapter 3: Sugar Free Cookie Recipes

Cinnamon Cookies

Ingredients

2 large eggs

2 tablespoons water

5 teaspoons granulated sugar replacement

1 teaspoon ground cinnamon

1 1/2 cup all-purpose flour

1/2 teaspoon baking soda

1/4 teaspoon salt

Directions

Preheat oven to 375°F (190°C).

Beat eggs and water in mixing bowl until light and fluffy. Beat in sugar replacement and cinnamon.

Combine flour, baking soda and salt in sifter; sift half of the dry ingredients over egg mixture. Fold to completely blend. Repeat with remaining dry ingredients.

Drop by teaspoonfuls onto greased cookie sheets, 2 to 3-inches apart.

Bake for 10 to 12 minutes.

Pumpkin Cookies

Ingredients

1/2 cup margarine, softened

1 1/4 cups Equal (sugar substitute)

1 cup canned pumpkin

1 teaspoon orange extract

1 1/4 cups all-purpose flour

3/4 cup whole wheat flour

1 teaspoon baking soda

1/4 teaspoon salt

1 1/2 teaspoons ground cinnamon

1 teaspoon pumpkin pie spice

1/2 teaspoon cloves

1/2 cup reduced-fat sour cream

1/2 cup raisins, finely chopped

2 teaspoons grated orange rind

1/4 cup chopped pecans

3/4 cup plus 4 teaspoons Equal

Warm skim milk or water

Ground cinnamon

Directions

Beat margarine and 1 1/4 cups Equal until fluffy in large bowl; beat in pumpkin and orange extract.

Mix in combined flours, baking soda, salt, and spices alternately with sour cream. Mix in raisins, orange rind, and pecans.

Spoon batter by heaping teaspoons onto greased cookie sheets. Bake cookies in preheated 375°F (190°C) oven until browned, 10 to 12 minutes.

Mix 2 tablespoons 3/4 cup plus 4 teaspoons Equal with enough warm milk to make a thin glaze consistency; brush lightly on warm cookies and sprinkle with cinnamon. Cool on wire racks.

Gingersnap Cookies

Ingredients

2/3 cup Splenda

3/4 cup granulated sugar

2/3 cup unsalted butter

1/3 cup molasses

2 tablespoons canola oil

1/4 cup egg substitute

3 1/4 cups all-purpose flour

2 teaspoons baking soda

8 teaspoons ground ginger

1/2 teaspoon ground cloves

2 teaspoons ground cinnamon

Directions

Mix Splenda, sugar, butter, molasses and oil together in a medium mixing bowl. Mix on medium speed until creamy. Scrape sides of the bowl. Add egg and mix well. Add remaining ingredients and mix until blended.

Divide dough in half. Roll into logs approximately 1 1/2-inches wide and 14 inches long. Cover with plastic wrap and refrigerate for 3 hours or freeze for 1 1/2 hours or until firm.

Preheat oven to 350°F (175°C). Lightly oil cookie sheets.

Slice cookies approximately 1/4-inch thick. Place on prepared sheets.

Bake 10 to 12 minutes or until bottoms are lightly browned.

Peppermint Chocolate Cookies

Ingredients
Cookie:

2/3 cup light butter

2 ounces unsweetened chocolate, melted

3/4 cup Splenda

1/4 cup egg substitute

1/4 teaspoon mint extract

2 cups all-purpose flour

1 teaspoon baking powder

1/2 teaspoon baking soda

Filling:
1 (8-ounce) package fat free cream cheese

1 (8-ounce) package reduced fat cream cheese

1 teaspoon vanilla extract

1/3 cup Splenda

Garnish:
30 hard sugar free peppermint candies, very finely crushed

Directions
Blend together butter, melted chocolate, and Splenda in a medium sized mixing bowl. Blend well. Add egg substitute and mint extract. Mix briefly. Add remaining ingredients. Mix using low speed or by hand until dough is formed. Do Not over mix.

Remove dough from bowl and divide in half. Chill dough in refrigerator 30 minutes. Preheat oven to 350°F (175°C).

Roll out chilled dough on a floured work surface. Roll dough slightly less than 1/4-inch thick. Cut dough into small one- inch circles. Place on lightly oiled cookie sheet. Bake for 7 to 9 minutes.

Blend filling ingredients together. Set aside.

Sandwich the cookies with 3/4 teaspoon filling. Press together lightly. Spread any excess filling from the interior of the cookie around the outside of each cookie. This will help the crushed peppermint candies stick to the outside of the cookies.

Roll cookies in crushed peppermint candies, so that the sides of each cookie are completely coated. Chill until ready to serve.

Classic Peanut Butter Cookies

Ingredients

1/4 cup margarine, softened

1 cup creamy style peanut butter

1/4 cup egg substitute

2 tablespoons honey

1/2 teaspoon vanilla extract

1 cup Splenda

1 1/2 cups all-purpose flour

1/2 teaspoon baking soda

1/2 teaspoon salt

Directions

Preheat oven to 350°F (175°C).

Beat margarine and peanut butter in a large mixing bowl with an electric mixer until creamy, approximately 1 minute.

Add egg substitute, honey and vanilla. Beat on high speed for approximately 1 1/2 minutes.

Add Splenda and beat on medium speed until well blended, approximately 30 seconds.

Combine flour, baking soda and salt in a small mixing bowl. Slowly add flour mixture to peanut butter mixture, beating on low speed until well-blended, about 1 1/2 minutes. Mixture may be crumbly.

Roll level tablespoons of dough into balls and drop onto a lightly oiled or parchment lined sheet pan, two inches apart. Flatten each ball with a fork, pressing a crisscross pattern into each cookie. Bake 7 to 9 minutes or until light brown around the edges. Cool on wire rack.

Oatmeal Pumpkin Raisin Cookies

Ingredients

2 cups all-purpose flour

1 1/3 cups quick or old-fashioned oats

1 teaspoon baking soda

1 teaspoon ground cinnamon

1/2 teaspoon salt

1 cup butter or margarine, softened

1/2 cup Splenda

1/2 cup Splenda, packed

1 cup pure pumpkin

1 large egg

1 teaspoon vanilla extract

3/4 cup chopped walnuts

3/4 cup raisins

Directions

Preheat oven to 350°F (175°C). Spray baking pans with nonstick cooking spray; set aside.

Combine flour, oats, baking soda, cinnamon and salt in medium bowl. Beat butter, Splenda and Splenda brown sugar.

Blend in large bowl at medium speed until light and fluffy. Add pumpkin, egg and vanilla extract; mix well. Add flour mixture; mix well. Stir in walnuts and raisins. Drop by rounded tablespoons onto prepared baking sheets.

Bake 14 to 16 minutes or until cookies are lightly browned and set in centers. Cool on baking sheets for 2 minutes; remove to wire racks to cool completely.

Pinwheel Cookies

Ingredients

3 (1-ounce) squares semisweet sugar free chocolate

1 cup unsalted butter, softened

1 cup Splenda

2 large eggs

2 teaspoons vanilla extract

4 cups all-purpose flour

1 teaspoon baking powder

1/4 teaspoon salt

Directions

Beat butter at medium speed with an electric mixer in a large mixing bowl until creamy. Gradually add Splenda, beating well. Add eggs, one at a time, mixing well after each addition. Stir in vanilla.

Melt chocolate in a 1-cup glass measuring cup at HIGH in a microwave oven for 1 to 1 1/2 minutes or until melted, stirring twice. Set aside.

Combine flour, baking powder, and salt in a separate mixing bowl. Gradually add flour mixture to Splenda, beating until blended. Do not over beat. Divide dough into half. Stir melted chocolate into half of mixture.

Place dough on a lightly floured work surface.

Roll chocolate dough into 2 (8 x 9-inch) rectangles. Roll vanilla dough into 2 (8 x 10-inch rectangles) Place the vanilla layer on bottom so that it extends 1 inch beyond the chocolate layer; roll as for a jellyroll.

Wrap logs in plastic wrap and chill cookie dough for one hour or until slightly firm.

Preheat oven to 350°F (175°C). Lightly grease cookie sheets. Remove dough from refrigerator. Slice cookies 1/4-inch thick and place on prepared cookie sheets.

Bake 8 to 10 minutes or until edges of cookies are lightly browned. Cool slightly on cookie sheets; remove to wire racks to cool completely.

Made in the USA
Las Vegas, NV
03 January 2022